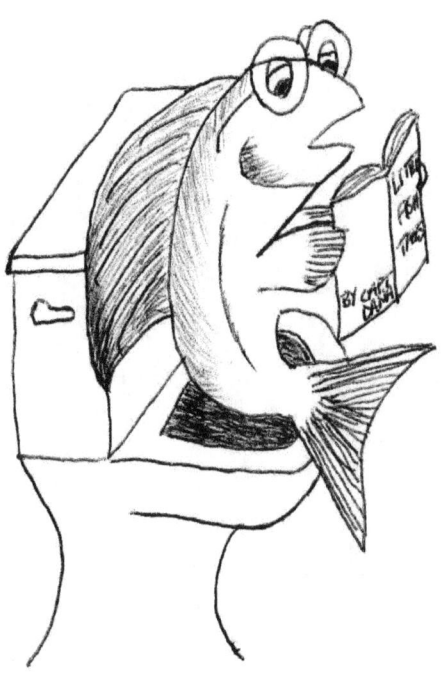

LITTLE FISH TAILS

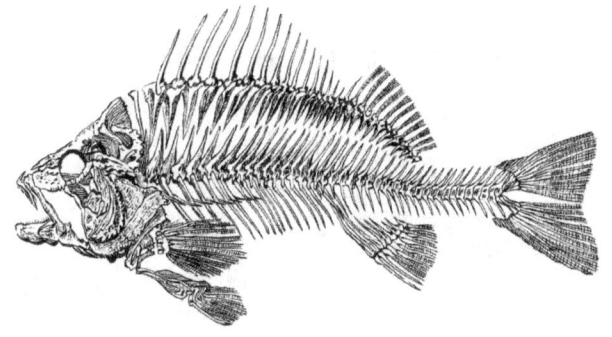

By
Captain Dana

Waughaw Press ©
P.O. Box 230
Palm Harbor, Florida 34682

Little Fish Tails

Copyright © 2001—2009 by Dana Price
All rights reserved, including the right to reproduce this book, or portions thereof, in any form

A Waughaw book.
Published by Waughaw Press
P.O. Box 230
Palm Harbor, Fl 34683

Book Design by ERROL WILLIAMS

Library of Congress Cataloging-in-Publication Data

Price, Dana
    Little Fish Tails / Dana Price
ISBN 978-0-9788122-1-8

First Edition: August 2009

Printed In the United States Of America

0 9 8 7 6 5 4 3 2 1

I dedicate this book to all who love fishing and the outdoors, and all my friends and family who have helped with this book.

Contents

Introduction

1. Fishing For Bar-B-Q
2. I'll Never Know
3. No Bull
4. Just Can't Take The Cold
5. A.K.A. Speck Hole
6. I'd Rather Be Lucky Than Good
7. Catching His Biggest
8. Fishing Adventure
9. Fishing Tackle Yard Sale
10. Fishing For Fun
11. Big Smalley
12. The Proof Is On The Wall
13. Never Give Up
14. Trout For Elk
15. First Cast
16. Size Does Matter
17. On An Indian Summer Afternoon
18. Cory's Little Pond
19. Telling Time
20. Sea Sick
21. Trained Bass
22. Just Lucky
23. Fishing In The Northwest Territories Of Canada

(A) Some Special Fish Recipes
    Pan Fry
    Ranch Broil
    Poor Man's Lobster

Little Fish Tails

This little book of stories is a light-hearted look at fishing. It is designed for reading while you are on the throne, or while you are waiting for the bride to come down the aisle. You shouldn't get too serious about fishing, because it is supposed to be fun.

1

FISHING FOR BAR-B-Q

It is difficult to keep your spouse happy and get in all the fishing you want. So, when my wife asked me on Wednesday if I would take her to a Saturday afternoon barbecue cook-off (her friend's husband was one of the contestants), I agreed since I figured this would be a good opportunity to score some positive points and make my wife more willing to let me go fishing at sometime in the future. As it happened, the very next morning, a co-worker asked me if I would take him fishing on Saturday. Since I had told him a few months earlier that "Anytime you want to go fishing, just let me know," I felt that I shouldn't put him off, because he might think my offer wasn't serious and he would never ask me again. So I told him I had to check with my wife to see what time we were supposed to arrive at the barbecue. She said "noon," so I asked if she would mind meeting me there so I could take my co-worker fishing on Saturday morning. She said, "O.K., but don't embarrass me by being late for the barbecue."

On Saturday morning, my friend and I met at the lake at about 5:30 a.m. so we could get in a good morning of fishing before I had to leave for the barbecue. The lake was about one hour away from where the barbecue was being held, so I told my friend I would have to leave by 11 in the morning. We fished until about 10:45 a.m. and, while I had pretty good luck, my co-worker had caught absolutely nothing. At that point, my co-worker reminded me that we should think about leaving so I could make it to the barbecue by noon. In the true fishing tradition, I said, "Let's fish just a few more minutes." Well, wouldn't you know it, the bass decided at that precise moment that it was time to go on the feed. We started catching fish on nearly every cast. As quick as we got our bait in the water we got another strike. No fisherman would, in good conscience, leave a hotspot when the fish are biting like that, so we continued fishing. Now, when I have a deadline to meet and the fish are really biting good (which seems to happen a lot), I often try to impose some discipline on myself by using the "10 cast rule" (if you cast 10 times and you do not get a strike, you quit). Well, that rule was obviously not going to work on this spot, so we decided to use the "5 cast rule." That didn't work either, so we soon got down to the "3 cast rule." After an hour-and-a-half of the best fishing I have ever had in my life, my friend said, "Dana, if you value your life, you had better get going to that barbecue, and by the way, you are already in BIG trouble with your wife." At that point my survival instinct took over, and I agreed.

I knew my co-worker liked to eat fish, so we had kept 2 limits of 10 bass each (this was a private lake in the middle of an orange grove so it was no big deal to keep so many fish). When we got to his car he told me what a great time he'd had, and said that I should just keep the fish because he didn't want to make me even later for the barbecue than I already was. I told him I would fillet the fish and give them to him later.

I got to the barbecue at 2:15 p.m. and was expecting an

outburst from my wife accusing me of being an insensitive lout. To my surprise, she greeted me happily with "Hi honey, how was your fishing?" My first thought was that aliens had taken over her body, but then I discovered that her friends had kept her so busy talking that she didn't know how late I really was. I also discovered that the husband of my wife's friend had won 1st place in the barbecued rib contest. He casually asked me if I had caught any fish, and I modestly told him "We did O.K." He asked if I had kept any, so I guided him over to my boat and showed him my livewell full of big bass. He said "How about trading some fish for ribs?" I asked him how many he wanted and he said "6 fillets about 1" thick would be nice." So I filleted 3 fish and in return, he gave me several slabs of ribs and said, "That's a good trade." Just then another guy who was a contestant at the barbecue saw what was going on and asked if he could get in on the "fish for ribs" deal. I said "Fine, but I'm not going to fillet any more fish." He said, "No problem, I'll fillet them myself." Then several other guys wanted to make the same kind of trade, and within a half-hour, I had traded all the fish for a stack of ribs about 18" high. My wife and I were eating ribs for a month. I also gave several slabs to my co-worker. Of course, I just had to take him fishing again to replace the fish he had caught on our first trip.

Some days everything goes right.

2

I'll Never Know

Up north in the spring, all the rivers are high and muddy because of the spring runoff. But I knew of a pay lake that was always clear because it was spring fed, and it did not get much runoff because it was in a pit. I decide to fish the lake because the local newspaper carried a story saying it had just been stocked with thousands of white bass. So I thought my chance for a good day of fishing was best there. I rented a small boat, and started cranking the bank. I caught a few fish, but it was pretty slow. In the late afternoon I went back to the dock and got some minnows to drag while I fished the shoreline. I put a minnow on a hook and let it free line. As the minnow worked its way down, I got a hit and caught a white bass. I started catching one after another until it was almost dark. Just then something big hit the minnow and the fight was on. I was using a fly rod with a 6 lb leader so I really had to play this monster. The fight went on into the night. It got so dark I could not see my hand in front of my face. Finally, the fish got tired and was laying on its side near the boat. But I couldn't see what it was, and I was afraid to lip it because there are muskies, pike and other toothy critters in the lake. I tried to lift the fish by the line to get a look at this behemoth. I had barely got the head out of the water when the line broke. It was so dark I could not see what it was. It was the biggest fish and the longest fight I ever had, and I will never know what it was.

I should have brought a flashlight.

3

No Bull

A friend and I fish a tributary of a small, pristine river. We call it a fishing adventure because we must navigate in small boats with outboards. We run in water so shallow we have to put the motor in shallow water drive and fix it so that when we hit logs, stumps, eel grass, downed trees, etc. the motor easily kicks up so the lower unit won't be damaged. As we slowly run upriver, the man in front of the boat fishes while the one in the back maneuvers over, under, around, and through the obstructions. On one such trip the water was very high and overflowing its banks into the woods, so we were able to get much farther upstream than usual. Many animals were seeking dry ground trying to get away from the water. All of a sudden my buddy says, "Look at the balls on that bull!" While I was still trying to understand what he had said, he changed his mind and said, "Bull, hell, that's a bear!" I looked up and saw a 500 to 600 lb black bear about 30 feet away. The bear looked at us without much concern. We continued on up the river and then started our float downstream. When we got back to the spot, he was still there without a care in the world, barely giving us a glance as we floated by. We have been back many times since and have never seen that big bear again.

And that's no bull.

4

JUST CAN'T TAKE THE COLD

Every fall I travel to just east of Indianapolis to visit my mother, siblings, and friends. I fish every morning and evening. My mother loves to eat fish so I stock her freezer while I'm there. My wife and daughters go on a week's vacation and they drop me off and I have to find a way home. After hearing stories for several years of all the smallmouth bass I catch on my trip, my buddy asked if he could pick me up this year. I said, "That's an 1800-mile round trip, and that's a long way to go to go fishing." He said that wasn't too far if the fishing is as good as I had been telling him. So we decided he would come. The weather had been great for my fishing time on the river, but the day before his arrival the weather turned cold. I had left some great spots unfished so when he arrived he would not have to fish places I had already pounded. Naturally, to get to the best spot we had to wade 3/8 of a mile through chest deep water. I am a freeze cat, but my friend isn't. By the time we got to the spot my teeth were chattering and I could not move. My friend said the cool air felt good after the hot summer months in Florida. I couldn't even think clearly, let alone fish because I was so cold. Luckily, I found a 10" round flat rock that was angled at the sun coming up over the trees. I laid there for about 45 minutes while my friend was catching smallies one after another. He kept saying, "Start fishing, they're biting great!" But I still could not move. Finally I warmed up enough to fish. He said I looked like a big alligator trying to warm up on that rock. We now call that rock "alligator rock."

He must have had a good time because he picked me up in Indiana for the next 3 years.

5

A.K.A. Speck Hole

I've fished tournaments for almost 30 years, but I don't fish them anymore. Some of my friends, though, have started fishing them now. In a recent tournament on Lake Okeechobee my friend Jimmy's wife did O.K., but he couldn't catch a fish big enough to measure. On their way home, they stopped in at our place to spend the night and I talked them into fishing a small river to improve his luck. We can only fish 2 per boat, so I got my friend Tommy to take Jimmy while I took Shirley, his wife. Tommy had decided to do it up right and make a shore lunch. I let Tommy go first so Jimmy would get the first shot at the best spots. I moved slowly, fishing a spot here and there to let Tommy's boat get ahead of us.

Now, in almost 30 years of fishing this river with Tommy, we have only caught about 6 specks (crappie) between us. On that day, Shirley and I came to a spot we call the "gar hole" because anytime you go there, you will see big schools of small gar. As I looked under the boat I saw a nice bass, so I tied up to an overhanging tree branch to fish slow in the current so the bait could get close to the bottom. Shirley was fishing a tube jig and I tied on a small gold spoon. In just a few casts I hooked up with a 6 lb bass. Shirley was also getting strikes, but she could not hook any fish. So I threw the gold spoon toward the spot where Shirley was getting strikes, thinking that maybe there were smaller bass there. As soon as the spoon hit the water, I hooked a speck. On each subsequent cast, I hooked another one. I asked Shirley if she wanted to try for them, and soon she was also catching one after another. All of these specks were nice fish—about 1 to 1 ½ lbs—so we decided to keep some. Tommy had brought redfish for lunch but I knew he would want some of these great tasting specks. It was getting close to lunch time, so I called the other boat on my cell phone to see when and where lunch would be. Shirley asked Jimmy how they were doing. He said it was a little slow. Shirley could not contain herself and told Jimmy how we were tearing up the specks. I could hear Tommy in the background muttering "We never catch specks up here." They were not too far from us, and said they would see us in a few minutes. They finally got within shouting range and Tommy said, "Don't give me that bull about the specks! And by the way, it'll be awhile before we eat because I forgot to get the red fish out of the cooler and they are still frozen." Shirley and I lifted four of the biggest specks out of the livewell and I said, "Does this look like bull? Not only that, they don't need to be thawed." Tommy, Jimmy and Shirley all agreed it was the best shore lunch they had ever had.

Now we call the gar hole A.K.A speck hole.

6

I'd Rather Be Lucky Than Good

I am a fishing guide in Central Florida. I know what I am doing, and think I'm a pretty good guide, but I still have lots to learn. Sometimes clients think guides are truly all-knowing about fishing. I once guided two bass fishermen from Indiana and we had a good day's fishing. We had put about 25 bass in the boat by 10 a.m., but as the morning wore on the bites slowed appreciably. I had stopped fishing early in the trip because they did not need me beating the water to a foam up ahead of them. By 11 a.m., they hadn't caught a fish in about 45 minutes. I said, "If you two don't get a fish soon, I'll have to show you how it is done." They sang out almost in unison, "Go ahead, show us what we are doing wrong." I picked up my rod and proceeded to catch 5 bass on 5 casts. They both thought that was amazing. I thought (but never said) how lucky I had been, and I didn't make another cast the rest of the trip. I made believers out of them and I knew better than to push my luck.

I'd rather be lucky than good.

7

Catching His Biggest

I took a Canadian pilot to a lake about an hour's drive out of Orlando because a cold front had moved through and I thought that lake might produce some good fish under rather tough weather conditions. He said he really wanted to get a 5 ½ lb largemouth bass because his biggest bass to date was a 5 ¼ lb smallmouth. I told him there were plenty of fish that size and bigger, and that we just needed a little luck to get what he wanted. We fished from one end of that chain of lakes to the other and caught a dozen or so bass, but the biggest was only 3 lbs. By then it was getting late and we had to start back. I planned to hit the best spots from earlier in the day and make a few casts in each spot. After cranking the motor up and planing the boat, I noticed a spot where I'd had good luck fishing in the past so on a hunch I turned to the right and shut the motor off. I jumped to the front of the boat, put the trolling motor down and told him that even though we hadn't tried this spot earlier, I had a good feeling about it. He started casting and on the third cast he hooked a nice fish. It got up in the weeds, so I told him to put heavy pressure on the fish and try to pull it out of the weeds. The bass jumped and came loose from the weeds and he worked it into the boat. We weighed it and it came in at 5 ½ lbs. I don't know how I could have been any luckier. He said that fish turned his trip from good to great.

You've got to go with your instincts.

8

Fishing Adventure

As a fishing guide, I take all kinds of people fishing. Sometimes if just one person wants to go out, I ask them if they want to just go fishing or if they want to go on a real fishing adventure. One such trip was an elderly gentleman named Kennedy. He looked like he was in good shape, but I asked him if he would have any trouble getting in and out of the boat. He said he would do fine. Before I left the house I called a friend that goes down the river a lot and told him I would be there with a client. He asked, "Do you want me to make a shore lunch?" I said "Sure, name the time and place." Kennedy and I where out early and had caught quite a few fish by lunch time. When we met my friend for lunch, he had everything set up and our lunch was waiting for us when we pulled up. We had a great lunch and shot the breeze a while. I asked if he wanted me to help clean up, but he said he could handle it, so Kennedy and I headed out again. After a couple more hours of fishing Kennedy started to tire. I asked if he was ready to quit. He said he was, so I started to square things up and asked if he had a good time. He looked at me and said, "I had only dreamed of a trip like this; thank you so much for a wonderful day. And please tell your friend I really enjoyed the shore lunch." Kennedy has written me a couple of times and sent some pictures. His health is failing and that was probably the last adventurous trip he could take.

He said he would remember it forever.

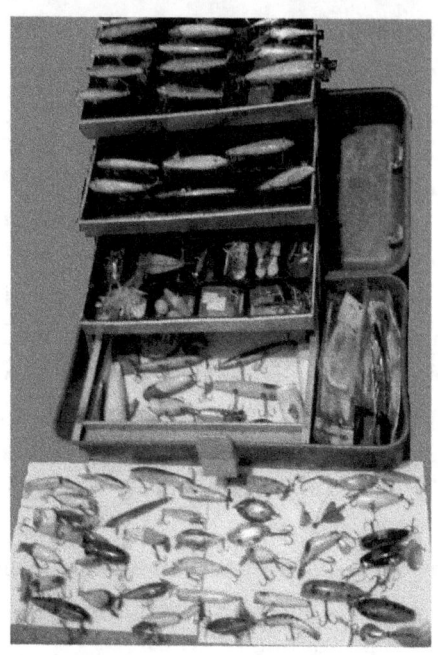

FISHING TACKLE YARD SALE

My wife is always wanting me to go to garage sales. We were on a weekend getaway at Cedar Key and about to leave the island when she spotted a yard sale sign. She said "Turn here." I didn't want to go, so I drove past the sale hoping she wouldn't see anything of interest. But instead she said "There's a tackle box you might want!" I thought she was just saying that to make me stop, but then I saw something that looked like it could be a tackle box, so I turned around and parked. As I walked toward the sale, I could see an old box with some rusted salt water lures. While I was looking at the baits my wife asked "How much for the lures?" Someone said "I think the owner wants a buck or two." My wife said "For each bait?" She was told "I don't know, ask the lady over there." When she asked the lady how much she wanted for the lures, she said "Take the whole box for a couple of bucks." The box contained mostly salt water lures and they were in pretty poor shape, but I thought for 2 bucks I couldn't go wrong.

When I got the box home, I took all the lures out of the box and put them into a sink full of warm soapy water and let them soak. After a while, I started cleaning them one at a time. There must have been 20 mirror lures that were worth $2 each. There were also several spoons with feathers, and after looking in my old lure book I discovered they were worth $20 to $30 each. There were also a dozen crank baits, some of which looked hand made. I thought they could be worth $150 to $200. Finally, there were a dozen other baits that were worth a total of $150 to $200. My wifes $2 tackle box treasure was worth over $500!

So now anytime she wants to go a garage sale, she says we might find another old tackle box. But I always tell her, that only happens once in a life time.

10

FISHING FOR FUN

It was a beautiful fall morning and a great day to hit the river. Eight of us were going to float our favorite spot to see what was biting. I was one of the old timers on the trip and I like to show the young bucks there's more to fishing than just setting the hook and slamming the fish into the boat. I had gone through my tournament days and had "been there, done that," so when we were pairing up for the float I asked my friends son if he would like to go with me. He said "O.K." and I told him I would like to show him there is more to fishing than catching. I said I wasn't going to try to catch any fish, but that I was looking for the 10 biggest strikes he had ever seen on the river.

Now, you need to know that his parents live across the highway from this river and he has been able to fish it all his life. But, as a tournament fisherman he spends a lot of time pre-fishing the area lakes and bigger rivers and doesn't fish this smaller river very often. The technique I was going to use is a soft plastic buzzing system a friend and I had developed several years earlier. The group started downstream in 4 canoes, with my young friend and I bringing up the rear. The trip was supposed to take about 6 hours and we planned to stop and fish rapids along the way, stretch our legs, and swap stories. We didn't catch up with the others until about 3 hours downstream, and when we got out of our canoe my partner started telling the others that I wouldn't set the hook on any fish and it was driving him nuts. Just then my brother in law said "I heard him tell you all he wanted was the 10 biggest strikes you ever saw." How many strikes did he get? My young friend replied "I quit counting at 12." Another voice rang out, "I guess he's accomplished his goal for today." I told my partner I was just trying to make a point—you don't have to catch them all to have a great day on the water. By the end of the day I had caught my share of the fish and I hope that I had made my point.

Fishing is about having fun, not just catching fish.

11

Big Smalley

It was a beautiful spring afternoon so I decided to go fishing. I called a few fishing buddies and they were all busy so I decided to go by myself. I took a blow-up, 2-man raft so I could anchor in a deep pool. I fished for a couple of hours with little success, but as evening approached, the action picked up. I was paddling the raft and casting to the rocky edges. Then I got a little tap. I waited for the line to tighten then set the hook. When I did, all hell broke loose. The fish started pulling my little raft all over that pool and then started jumping. It was a 7 to 8 lb smalley. I had never seen one that large. After jumping, he went back down and pulled me around some more. Then I could feel this monster starting to tire (so was I!). Then, he made one last spectacular jump just inches from my tiny rubber boat and dove under the boat; then the line went slack. I sat there in disbelief. No one but me saw the fish, but I know it happened.

    I hope you believe me...??

12

THE PROOF IS ON THE WALL

My brother in law, John, and I had made plans to go fishing on a Saturday morning in May. I had an 8' fiberglass dingy with an electric trolling motor. We were going to East Lake Toho and fish the boat runs because we didn't think it would be a good idea to fish the big open water in such a small boat. For most of the morning, fishing was very slow and we only had a couple of bites between us. We decided to quit because the wind had picked up and the fish weren't biting. I made a long cast down a boat run, but my bait was blown 10 feet to the right and landed on a big mat of heavy weeds. I thought "That's great! The wind's blowing so hard I can't even hit the open water." Just then, the grass mat exploded. I dropped the rod tip then set the hook. The fight was on. I gradually worked that big bass out of the heavy cover. He jumped one time in the mat and swam to the weeds like a mono weed wacker. He spun the dingy 180 degrees, got into the open water, and then jumped again. I knew I had him now because he couldn't get back into the weeds. Or so I thought. Within seconds, he spun the boat another 180 degrees and was back in the heavy grass in a flash. I pulled, he pulled, I pulled, he pulled. Finally he came out of the grass mat. John asked "Do you want me to net him?" I said "Only if you can get a clear shot at him." Just then the fish came by the boat, and with one swoop John had him in the net. Long story short: this ain't no fish story, the proof is on the wall.

That fish was 27 ½" long, and it was the only bass we caught that day.

13

Never Give Up

I was a superintendent for an HVAC contractor and fished some tournaments on weekends. The owner of the company (Ron) expressed an interest in fishing a tournament, so when I was asked to fish a small event I asked Ron if he wanted to fish with me. We were not able to pre-fish at all because it was too far to travel after work. On the day of the tournament, I was just going to look for submerged vegetation and lily pads as these areas always hold fish. I also looked for a fishing spot that was in sight of the weigh-in area, so if we couldn't get our motor started we could get a tow or troll to the weigh-in.

It was a tough day, and nobody was getting many hits. We had two small keepers, but it didn't look good. My partner was getting antsy even though there were still a couple of hours of fishing time left. He was ready to throw in the towel because he didn't think we had much chance to place in the money. I told him "You always fish to the end." I also told him there was a little island in sight of the weigh-in area, and that we would be fishing there until the last minute. Reluctantly he agreed. A bit later we went to the island. On the fourth or fifth cast I hooked a 3½ lb largemouth. It was a great fight and I was being very careful to make sure I landed the fish. Shortly thereafter we started up the motor and ran to the weigh-in. I like to hold back until others weigh in or until I see that my catch will not make a difference. But on this day, I watched many anglers weigh in and no one had a bigger fish than our biggest. Their totals were also small. I also noticed another pair holding back, so I was hoping it would come down to our two teams. They were the local team, so we weighed in first. When we picked our big bass out their jaws dropped, not that it was that big, but they could see it was at least ½ lb bigger than their biggest. We only had 3 fish for a total of 6½ lbs. They had a 5 fish limit of 4 very small fish and a 3 pounder as their anchor for a total of 7¼ lbs. They got the win and won $325. We got 2nd place and big fish and collected $575 for the day. My teammate said, "I learned something about tournament fishing. If you're having a tough day it might be tough on every one and it only takes one cast to get you in the money."

He's been hooked on tournament fishing ever since and finished in 10th place on the co-anglers side in a big B.A.S.S. event.

14

TROUT FOR ELK

If you work in construction, sometimes you have to travel long distances to get work when work is slow in your area. One time my friend Rick and I traveled to Idaho to look for work and do a little trout fishing. A few years earlier, Rick had befriended a co-worker when he worked in Alaska on the oil pipeline close to Prudhoe Bay, and he said we could stay with his co-worker while we were in the Boise area. When we arrived, we asked Rick's friend if there was a place close by that we could do a little trout fishing. He said there was a small creek called Morris Creek that we could wade, and gave us directions. The next morning at breakfast his wife made a wonderful breakfast that included eggs, potatoes, biscuits, gravy, sausage, bacon, and elk tenderloin. I had never had elk tenderloin and really liked it .We asked our host if he wanted us to bring trout for dinner. He said that would be great, but they would not count on us to supply the entree because the native trout were not easy to catch, and a couple of rookies like us would have a tough time. Teasingly he said "How about us trading elk tenderloin for trout?" They had plenty of elk in the freezer and no trout. Anyway, Rick's friend went to work and we headed to Morris Creek.

Within an hour we had discovered a pattern: make long casts with a #2 bucktail Mepps to the bends in the creek into little eddies. In almost every eddy there were 1 or 2 fish. We made little stringers and staked out our fish as we leapfrogged each other fishing downstream. When we both had limited out (which was 10 fish each), we worked back up the creek and collected our catch. When we returned to Rick's house, he and his wife were anxious to see our catch. We said "Get your elk ready to trade." They thought we might have caught a few trout, since we had been out most of the day. But they were not prepared for the size of our stringer. We started out by showing our smallest trout (which were 2 inches bigger than the minimum) and worked our way up to the biggest. We could have cleaned out our host of his elk, but after the trading was over we gave them all the fish. They said they had enough trout to last through the winter.

They said they would not doubt our fishing skills (luck) again.

15

First Cast

My friend 'The Berman' wanted me to take him fishing for a couple of hours one day. So I met him at his house and we loaded the boat with fishing tackle and drinks. Then took off to the ramp, which was just around the corner from his house, launched the boat and headed for one of our favorite spots. On the very first cast, The Berman hooked a monster bass. The fight was on. The fish jumped, swam through some lily pads, popped out into open water, jumped again, then back into the weeds, then back out to open water. Finally, he got the fish close enough for me to get a lip lock on him and I lifted a 9 ½ lb large-mouth bass into the boat. With that, The Berman said: "Well that's all I came for, let's go home." After the trip, my friend estimated the total cost of the trip to be just $1.75, and that included a Pepsi.

Too bad it's not always that easy or cheap.

16

SIZE DOES MATTER

One beautiful summer morning a client brought his wife along with him so she would not have to stay in the motel room by herself. She wasn't really interested in fishing. I told her I would give her fishing lessons for free. She agreed, since she "never passed up anything for free." I started with the basics: how to hold the rod and reel, how to hold the line with your finger on the reel, the proper casting motion, and when to release the line. It was plain to see she was a natural. She had listened to all of my instructions and was casting quite well within 15 minutes. The next step was to show her how to work the bait. A soft plastic is one of the easiest baits to work because you almost can't work it wrong. If the fishing is real good, you can fish it fast or slow and fish will hit the bait. But if the fishing is slow, then you slow the retrieve way down. Well, the bite that day was a little slow. I kept reminding her husband to slow down his retrieve, but his nature was to work too fast. But his wife did slow it down as I had told her, and pretty soon she started getting bites. By the time the first hour was up, she had caught several nice bass and her husband had only caught one small one. As the morning progressed, she continued to outfish her husband, and was catching fish up to 4 pounds. Her husband was only picking up a small one here and there. He simply would not slow down his retrieve enough to get the bigger bites. Several hours passed, and now we were getting close to the end of the trip. Her husband hooked another small bass and I reached down to pick it up. It was a perfect specimen: pure white belly, differing shades of green markings on the sides, and almost pure black on his back. I offered the opinion that the color of the fish was beautiful and they both agreed. I said to the woman, "Isn't this the prettiest fish we've caught today"? The wife had caught the biggest fish, the most fish, and the very first fish, so she had beat her husband in all categories, but I was just trying to acknowledge that he too had something to brag about. She looked at the fish, then at her husband, back at the fish, then back at her husband and finally said: "OK, that is the prettiest fish of the day." But I wasn't convinced her comment was heartfelt.

With that I threw it back into the water and said: "Yes, it was pretty, but I guess in fishing, SIZE DOES MATTER."

17

On An Indian Summer Afternoon

One summer day, a friend and I got off work a little earlier than usual and decided to take his 5 year old son fishing for catfish on the Great Miami River. We got our gear together, loaded the truck and were off to the bait shop. We got a couple dozen night crawlers and headed to the river. It wasn't long after, we cast our worms out, that we had our first catfish. We caught several small ones and then a small carp. Just then my friend's rod started heading south, and he was lucky to grab it before it went into the water. We were using light tackle so it was a great fight. He landed a 7 lb channel cat. With that, his son Wayne got very nervous and it was clear that he was afraid of that large fish. We tried our best to calm him down, but Wayne wanted nothing to do with the big fish. But I had a backup plan. I told my friend to get Wayne away from the fish and get him focused on a hawk that had landed on a nearby tree. While he was occupied, I hooked the big cat onto Wayne's line, and let the fish back into the water. I hollered to Wayne: "I think you are getting a bite you better get to your pole." He hurried over and felt his line then hollered to his Dad: "I got a bite." He set the hook as best he could, not knowing I had buried the hook in the cat's tough mouth. Wayne fought his fish with all his might and finally landed that 7 pounder. With that, he exclaimed: "Dad, my fish is bigger than yours!"

All his fears about big catfish had suddenly vanished once the fish was HIS.

18

Cory's Little Pond

My nephew Cory lives in the country outside Indianapolis. There is a small pond on the farm and he and his grandfather fish it once in a while and catch pan fish. They typically use red worms on small hooks with floaters. I asked Cory if there was big bass in the pond, but because they had only fished for pan fish, he didn't know. So I went down to the pond with a bait that I had developed with a friend of mine to try my luck for bass. It is a soft plastic bait that I like to buzz across the top of the water and vegetation. The fish really liked that bait, and it didn't take me long to start catching bass. When I was finished, I went back to the house and told Cory I had caught a bunch of nice bass. He immediately wanted to go to the pond and see how I was catching bass. My first cast was at an angle to the bank over some duckweed. I had not moved the bait more than ten feet when all hell broke loose. A big bass exploded on the bait. I dropped the bait back then set the hook as hard as I could. The fight was on… jumping, thrashing, pulling, just a great bass fight. When it was over, we weighed the fish: 6 pounds. Cory said that was the biggest bass he had ever seen. I threw about 15 more times and caught ten more bass.

You can bet that Cory looked at that pond a little differently after seeing the difference between bass and pan fish.

19

TELLING TIME

I was guiding a client on a bass fishing trip and he asked me what time it was. I thought this was a little strange, since he had a watch on and I didn't. What he didn't know was that I had left a hatch on the boat open next to me, to let it dry out, and I had my pager in the hatch, which displayed the time. When he asked me what time it was, I surreptitiously looked in the hatch, saw the time and then pretended to look into the sky as if I was reading the time from the sun. I then told him the time, to the minute. As it happened, the fish were really on the feed that day, so we were getting plenty of strikes and boating a lot of fish, but for some reason he kept asking the time about every half-hour. I would take a quick look in the hatch and then gaze at the position of the sun and then tell him the time to the minute. This was an all-day trip, so he asked me for the time 10 or 12 times during the next several hours. Each time I went through the same routine. As the trip was coming to an end, he asked one last time and I gave it to him right on the money again. With that he said, "You know Captain Dana, you have an uncanny ability to tell the time by the sun. Acting surprised, I said "I do"? I never told him about the hatch with the pager sitting inside. I'm waiting for another client who will ask me whether I can tell time by the sun.

If I do it on a cloudy day, the client will be even more impressed.

20

Sea Sick

At one point in my career, I was a general superintendent for a large sheet metal contractor. One day a contractor that we did work for asked my wife and I to go on a deep sea fishing trip. As an avid tournament and weekend fisherman, I was more than happy to go on this offshore trip. We met him at his penthouse suite in a condo on Singer Island in south Florida. What a beautiful place, with the intracoastal waterway to the west and the Atlantic Ocean to the east. We arrived in the evening, so we went out to dinner and had a great meal. Upon our return, we looked at the weather forecast, which did not look good. (8-10 foot seas which would make it difficult to fish). We weren't even sure if we should go out and try our luck. So, we decided to wait until the next morning and see how things looked. One of the other guys that was supposed to go on the trip was prone to seasickness, so he decided to take a pill just in case. My wife also took a pill that night in anticipation of the rough seas in the morning. She also began bugging me to take a pill as well. But I told her that I had been in rough seas before and had never gotten seasick. Besides, I didn't want to take a pill. She kept bugging me about how hardheaded I was, and asked what would it hurt to take a pill to be on the safe side? She said it was the non-drowsy formula and it would not bother me. I finally relented and took the pill just before I went to bed. The next morning we got up, had breakfast and decided to try fishing. The seas were rough, but it looked like we would be able to fish. I was still a little groggy from the "non-drowsy" pill. I don't normally take any pills so I knew it would affect me more than the average person.

When we got to the boat, I saw that it was a great looking 48' sport fisherman with a flying bridge. When we got aboard, we saw that it had all the first class amenities: big screen T.V., sound system, leather seats, and a Marlin in the coffee table. We headed out, and I just could not get my head together. By the time we were offshore I could not get off the couch. Everyone was on the back deck and I was still on the couch. I wasn't sick; I just couldn't get up. Over the next little while, each guest caught a fish, so then it was my turn. I struggled back to the fighting chair and started reeling in a fish (luckily it was a small barracuda). I cranked him in as fast as I could and went right back to the couch. My wife was laughing at me the whole time. I don't drink alcohol, but she said I looked like I was drunk. The seas were too rough for us to stay out very long. We were back for a couple of hours before I started feeling myself again.

I will never ever take another seasickness pill. Never!

21

Trained Bass

A couple of my friends are avid fishermen, and they have a small pond on their property in Ohio. I live in Florida, and everyone knows that bass are bigger in Florida than they are in Ohio. When my friends visited me, I took them fishing. They caught a couple of nice bass which they decided to take home and throw into their little pond. It was winter so the fish traveled well in the cold water. When they got home, they added water from their pond to their live well to get them use to the new water. When the fish were released into the pond they swam away. Over the next few weeks, my friends saw the fish swimming around in their pond. They were easy to spot, because they were by far the biggest bass in the pond. When spring came, they dug up worms and threw them to the big fish to help them get even bigger. Pretty soon the fish learned that when my friends splashed their hands in the water, it was time to eat. It got to the point that when they splashed their hands in the water, the bass would come over and take the worms right out of their hand (like you see the big bass do when they feed them minnows at

Bass Pro Shops). They just loved their big Florida fish.

A couple of years went by and the bass were still doing well. I went up to visit them and had a new bait to show them so we went down to the pond and I told him how to work the new bait. My friend cast way out into the pond and as soon as the bait hit the water the biggest of his Florida bass pounded the bait. He could not believe it, but one of the only two fish he did not want to hit had devoured the bait. He started hollering: "Take the rod! Take the rod! I don't want the fish to know I'm the one who hooked her!" With that, I took the rod and worked the fish in as gently as I could, took her off and returned her to the pond, trying not to stress her out any more than necessary.

My friend was almost in tears and vowed never to cast into the pond again.

22

Just Lucky

A friend of mine called me and asked if I wanted to try our luck on the lake for a couple of hours. My wife and I were just watching TV and for me, doing anything outdoors (especially fishing) beats watching TV any time. So my friend came over and the three of us launched an 8-foot dingy with a trolling motor in a small bay of a big lake. We went all around the bay and had a few bites, but could not seem to hook anything. My wife was not really into fishing, but she half-heartedly threw out a line. I told her to watch it because she just might get a big one. An hour went by and nothing happened. Just then I saw the line on my wife's rod start twitching. I did not tell her I saw a hit. I just said she should check her bait. She casually picked up the rod and slowly cranked in a little line. Then she said, "I think I feel a bite." I told her to tighten up the slack and set the hook. My wife reared back hard and set the hook, and it was immediately apparent that it was a good-sized fish. In fact, the fish was big enough that it was taking out line even thought the drag was set pretty tight. Then my wife said to me, "Take the rod, the fish is too big for me to get in." About that time, the fish jumped and I could see that it was about 7 pounds. I told her to just keep reeling and she would catch the biggest fish she had ever caught. So, she kept cranking until she got the fish close to the boat, and I reached down and pulled the fish out of the water She was pretty excited and relieved that we had landed the fish. By this time it was getting close to dark, so I said we had better start heading in. I just couldn't help myself, but I had to make a few more casts on the way in. I took the rod she had just caught the big one on and started casting to a dock on the way in. Just then a big fish crashed the same bait that the 7 pounder had hit. I set the hook and the fight was on. This fish was pulling harder than the one my wife had gotten and was taking a lot of line off the reel. I kept working it and finally I could feel the fish tiring. The bass made one final jump, and I could see that it was even bigger than the fish my wife had just caught. I finally landed the fish and weighed it: 9 pounds! At that point, my wife muttered, "Can't you let me beat you at fishing just ONE time?"

I tried to explain that it was just pure luck, but she will always believe I just had to top her.

23

Fishing In The Northwest Territories Of Canada

My friend Jerry and I used to go fishing in the Northwest Territories of Canada every summer. We would fly from Winnipeg, Manitoba to Neultin Lake, which straddles the border of Manitoba and the Northwest Territories. Our goal was to catch big lake trout. The fishing on the lake was usually excellent, and we caught many fish between 15 and 40 pounds in the course of a week's fishing. But one year, we had real trouble catching big fish, so we asked the camp manager if he had any ideas. He said, "Go up to Bemidji Point because at this time of the year the big trout congregate up there in about 40 feet of water." So, bright and early the next morning we headed off to Bemidji Point, which was about 15 miles up the lake (the lake is over 100 miles long). When we arrived on the spot, I put on an 8-ounce in-line sinker to get my big red-and-white spoon down near the bottom. Jerry didn't put on a sinker since he doesn't like to fish with big sinkers. We started trolling, and in about 10 SECONDS I had a strike. After fighting the fish for about 20 minutes, I finally got it to the surface and we boated the fish. It weighed 25 pounds. I told Jerry that he should put on a big sinker because apparently all the big trout were near the bottom. But he said he didn't like those big sinkers and he would stick with just the big spoon. So, we started trolling again, and in about one MINUTE I got another big strike. After another long fight, we boated a 37 pound lake trout.

That was enough for Jerry. He started to put a big sinker on his line, but then he said, "You know, I'm not feeling too well. Take me up to the shore and I'll lie down awhile. I'll let you know when I'm ready to come back out and fish." So, I took him up to the shore and then went back out fishing. Almost immediately, I hooked another big lake trout. There must have been a lot of big trout on the bottom at that spot in the lake. Anyway, over the next few hours I hooked a bunch of big lake trout, but Jerry still wasn't feeling well enough to come back out fishing. Finally, he said he wanted to go back to camp, so he got back in the boat and we motored back to the camp. He said, "We've got to go back to Bemidji Point tomorrow when I'm feeling better, because I want to catch some of those big trout. I said, "I'm all for that. Let's do it."

Well, sometimes things don't work out. The next day (and the rest of the week, for that matter) the wind was so high that we never did get back to Bemidji Point.

Appendix

Some Special Fish Recipes

No book on fishing stuff would be complete without a couple of fish recipes. Most of my friends and family love these.

Pan Fry

Make a milk and egg wash mixture (scramble a couple of eggs and add a little milk) in a bowl. Put the fish into the mixture for a few seconds, take it out and let drain for a couple of seconds, and put a sprinkle of season salt on one side. Then put it in a plastic baggie (large one) with Italian bread crumbs (Progresso is a good brand). Shake the fillets, then pan fry in hot peanut oil and cook until they are golden brown. Put the fillets on paper towels to drain and cool for a couple of minutes. Then dig in. Great with cole slaw and french fries. Great for a shore lunch.

Ranch Broil

This one is even easier but it tastes like you spent a lot of time preparing. Cut fillets into finger size pieces. Put them into a glass baking dish suitable for oven and microwave, cover the fish with ranch dressing and sprinkle on some paprika. Put in the microwave oven until the fish is cooked (it turns white and flaky). Then put it under the broiler until the top turns golden. People will be begging for this one. You can use your favorite dressing (instead of ranch) with this recipe.

Poor Man's Lobster

Cut fish into pieces about the size of big lobster claws or whatever size suits the fish you are cutting. Boil fish until the fish oil comes out, not too long though because some fish will fall apart. (Note: if it is a mild tasting fish already then no need to boil.) Next, place the fish into a pan and cook in butter and garlic or extra virgin olive oil and garlic until it starts to turn brown. Drain on a paper towel. Dip into drawn butter (dip as you would lobster).

THE END

You may contact Captain Dana at:

Captain Dana Price
2360 Clay Court
Longwood, FL 32779
407-645-5462

Or email him at:
captdana1@aol.com

www.ingramcontent.com/pod-product-compliance
Lightning Source LLC
LaVergne TN
LVHW021736060526
838200LV00052B/3300